The New Kid at School

by Lisa Oram

PEARSON

Scott
Foresman

Editorial Offices: Glenview, Illinois • Parsippany, New Jersey • New York, New York
Sales Offices: Needham, Massachusetts • Duluth, Georgia • Glenview, Illinois
Coppell, Texas • Ontario, California • Mesa, Arizona

Every effort has been made to secure permission and provide appropriate credit for photographic material. The publisher deeply regrets any omission and pledges to correct errors called to its attention in subsequent editions.

Unless otherwise acknowledged, all photographs are the property of Scott Foresman, a division of Pearson Education.

Photo locators denoted as follows: Top (T), Center (C), Bottom (B), Left (L), Right (R), Background (Bkgd)

Cover: ©Will & Deni McIntyre/Corbis; 1 ©George Shelley/Corbis; 5 ©Patrick Bennett/ Corbis; 6 ©George Shelley/Corbis; 7 ©Yellow Dog Productions/The Image Bank/ Getty Images; 8 ©Michael Keller/Corbis; 9 ©Charles Gupton/Corbis; 11 ©Will & Deni McIntyre/Corbis; 13 ©Charles Gupton/Corbis; 14 ©Bob Rowan; Progressive Image/ Corbis; 15 ©Tom & Dee Ann McCarthy/Corbis; 16 ©Pete Saloutos/Corbis; 19 ©LWA-Dann Tardif/Corbis; 20 ©Michael Pole/Corbis; 22 ©Gabe Palmer/Corbis; 23 ©Will & Deni McIntyre/Corbis

ISBN: 0-328-13557-7

1 2 3 4 5 6 7 8 9 10 V0G1 14 13 12 11 10 09 08 07 06 05

Do you remember a time when you got a new pair of sneakers? Were you really excited? Had you wanted them for a long time? What was it like on the first day you wore them to school?

New shoes often mark the beginning of a new school year or the start of a sports season. If the shoes are a birthday present, you are beginning a new year in your life. If you have outgrown your old shoes, your body is different than it used to be. Shoes are just shoes, of course, but it seems that when they change, life is changing too.

Everybody experiences change—sometimes big changes and sometimes simple ones. Any change can bring with it a combination of opposite feelings.

You might be excited about the new thing, and you might also be nervous. You might be sad about something you are leaving or losing, while at the same time, you welcome a fresh start. You can toss your ratty old red sneakers and love your new green ones, but you'll probably never forget wearing that old pair when you broke the record for the 50-yard dash or on your first day at a new school.

Going to a new school is one of the biggest new beginnings there is. Whether it's moving from elementary school to middle school with all your friends, or moving to a new neighborhood in the middle of the school year, it's a big change.

In this book, you will explore the experience of going to a new school. If you are the kid who is new, there are things you can do to help yourself with the changes. If you are the kid who's been around for a while, there are things you can do to help a new kid feel welcome.

This is Marcus. He moved from a small town to a big city when he was in fifth grade because his father got a new job. He didn't want to move and was mad at his parents for a long time, but now he says it's better. He still misses his old school, but his new one feels okay. We are going to learn from him what it was like to be the new kid, how others helped him, and how he helped himself.

About his first day, Marcus says, "I was worried about a lot of things. The new school was much bigger than my old one, and I was scared of getting lost. I wondered if my new teacher would be strict or nice. I was afraid I would never make new friends or that other kids might be mean to me."

Knowing that a new student might feel the way that Marcus did, what could you do to help?

Introduce Yourself

Making friends is probably the biggest concern of someone who starts at a new school, especially if the person has moved from far away and doesn't know anyone at all. Make the first move. If you are sitting next to the person, say hello. At lunch, ask your new classmate to sit with you and your friends. Introduce all the kids around you to the newcomer.

Sometimes kids worry that a new friend will somehow take away the friends they already have. But, really, you can never have too many friends, and the new kid will surely appreciate your efforts.

You might feel shy or embarrassed talking to someone you don't know at all, but remember, the new kid is probably feeling a lot more worried than you.

Start a Conversation

If you don't know a person well, it might feel like you don't know what to talk about. In fact, not knowing someone means there's a lot to talk about. You don't know anything about that person so you can be curious and ask about almost anything.

You can start by finding out what your new friend likes to do. Does she play sports? Does she like to read or go bike riding? Does he like video games? Does he have any collections? Keep asking questions, and pretty soon you're sure to find something you have in common.

Kids come to a new school for lots of different reasons. The more you talk together, the more you'll find out about each other's lives. Sometimes kids end up in a new school because of difficult home situations. You may hit upon a topic that your new friend doesn't want to talk about.

Eventually, when you know each other better, you both will feel more comfortable talking about personal matters. In the meantime, if you feel awkward, just change the subject to something really silly like, "Wanna see my cavities?"

Be Prepared

One of the worst feelings when starting at a new school is the feeling that the people at the new school don't know what to do with you when you get there.

It's unsettling to see people scrambling around, asking, "Where does the new kid go?" It's embarrassing to arrive at your new classroom and wait around while a bunch of other kids move their seats so there's somewhere to sit. The last thing you want to hear from your new teacher is something like, "He's not supposed to be in my class. I thought he was supposed to go into the other fifth-grade class." If your class and your school do a little advance work, a new student's entry can be a whole lot nicer.

Marcus says, "At my new school, the assistant principal gave me a welcome kit on the first day. It was just a little bag of things, like a notebook, a pen, a map of the school, and a copy of the school newspaper. There was even a dollar in there so I could buy something in the cafeteria. I thought it was really nice."

Your class could also create a welcome gift, like a flower on the new person's desk or a special snack for the class that day.

You could create a book containing one sentence of advice from each student in the class. What other ideas do you have about doing something special to greet a new student in your class?

Be an Expert

Marcus not only had to change schools but he had to live in an apartment instead of a house and get to know a whole new town. His family had to figure out where the grocery store was, where the post office was, and who to choose as a new doctor. Marcus was on the basketball team at his old school, so he needed to find the coach at his new school.

When you're the old kid, you can be an expert. Offer the new kid a tour of your school or of your town. Point out the nurse's office, the library, or the gym as you walk between classes. Even if someone else has already given the tour, there are so many things for the new kid to remember at the beginning that your help will still feel useful. Another word for this kind of expert is *mentor*, someone more experienced than another person, who takes on the role of an advisor and a helper.

When you learn more about what your new classmate likes to do, offer suggestions that relate to his or her interests. If the new kid likes computers, or painting, or dance, but it's a subject that you don't know anything about, steer him or her to someone who does.

You also might have special insider information to share—like your teacher loves to watch reruns of Star Trek and asking about his favorite episode can delay a spelling quiz. Getting the inside scoop takes away the feeling of being an outsider.

If the new kid has changed schools within the same town, the new things to learn will be fewer than they were for Marcus. Still, you know things that the new kid doesn't, so you can lead the way.

If you are changing schools or moving into a new town, it's not only up to others to help you feel welcome. *You* need to help make the change successful. You may be a kid who's moved a lot, so you have a system. Maybe you lay low at the beginning and then slowly warm up. Maybe you go in wanting to make a strong impression right from the start. There's no right or wrong way. If you're moving to a new school for the first time, you will need to find the way to fit in that best suits your personality.

Remember, though, you were a new kid at least once before, when you started kindergarten. One way to help yourself is to think about that time, even though it may have been a long time ago, and remind yourself that you got through it. Way back then you didn't know anything about school at all. At least this time, you already know the basics.

Saying Good-Bye

Perhaps as important as being able to say hello is being able to say good-bye. As you are preparing for the change, it's tempting to ignore this part. You don't want it to happen, so maybe if you pretend it's not coming up, it will go away.

As much as possible, you need to say good-bye—to your friends, your teachers, your playground, your lunchroom. Sometimes a move comes up quickly, and you're not given much, or any, time to get ready. In that case, you can write and send a good-bye letter after you are gone. The people you have left also wanted to say good-bye, so a letter will help them too.

If you can, take photos or mementos with you to help you remember the place you are leaving. Make plans about how you can communicate after you've left, or when you might visit again. Keeping connections with parts of your past will ultimately make it easier in the long run to make similar connections in your future.

Show Off

Find an activity that demonstrates a special side of you or shows off your strongest skills and interests. Probably anything that you liked at your old school will be available at your new school, even if it's not offered in exactly the same form.

If you like playing soccer, ask about a school team. If you were in the photography club, and there isn't one at your new school, ask your teacher if there are other ways to use your skill. Perhaps there's a school newspaper or yearbook that needs photos. Maybe the principal likes to display photos of school events in the office or hallways. When you pursue your favorite activities, you will naturally meet other kids who share your interests and who could become new friends.

Be Yourself

Sometimes moving to a new school feels like an opportunity to reinvent yourself. Nobody knows you are a great singer, so if you don't want to join the chorus, you don't have to. Your new teacher has never given you a zero for not doing homework, and you can make it so he never does.

Marcus says, "I thought maybe I would tell people that my old house had burned down and that was why my family had to move. If the kids felt sorry for me, maybe they'd like me better. Or maybe they would just think it was interesting and want to talk to me."

The bottom line is that a fresh start is a chance to do things better, but you can't be anyone other than your true self. You have to be real and follow your heart. If some kids in your new school say, "Everyone around here cuts class, and it doesn't matter," but you think it's not right, don't be afraid to stand up for yourself. Those kids might not like you, but then ask yourself if those are the kids you really want to be friends with. There will be other kids who respect your courage and honesty. In the end, the only way to be happy is to be true to yourself.

Expect Ups and Downs

Fifth grade can be a year of many changes even without going to a new school. Becoming ten years old and moving into the double-digit period of life feels to many kids like the beginning of being a teenager. You want to be more independent. You want to experiment with different ways of acting around your peers, your parents, and your teachers. As the new kid, you have two sets of changes at the same time—the new place and new people on the outside, and your changing feelings on the inside.

In many schools, fifth graders are the oldest kids around, the ones with the most experience, but this profile changes quickly when they go off to middle school and become the youngest ones again. Knowing that they are soon to lose their status, some fifth graders want to make the most of their position while they can. Sometimes that means being bossy or excluding anyone who doesn't match their personal level of "cool."

No matter how prepared you try to be for all these changes, there are bound to be days when nothing feels right. Life was probably a little up and down before changing schools, and it won't be any different afterward. It helps to expect the ups and downs rather than imagining that everything is going to be perfect if you just... find a best friend, or ace the first test, or whatever.

No single thing is going to make everything at your new school great, and no single thing will make it all bad either. Realistic expectations will help you get through a process that takes time.

So, back to those sneakers from the beginning of this book. When a new student arrives at your school, try walking for a few minutes in his or her shoes. Step in and step up. You can show the new kid that your class is a great place to be. And you will have a new friend that might become your best one yet!

If you're the new kid, take a deep breath and start asking questions. Give yourself time. It's a little like getting new shoes. You need to break them in, but soon you will be able to hit your stride in them. Just as soon, you will have become used to the new school.

Glossary

cavities *n.* pitted areas in teeth that are caused by decay and often filled in by a dentist.

combination *n.* the joining of two or more separate things.

demonstrates *v.* shows clearly.

episode *n.* one part in a series of related parts; often refers to dramatic performances such as television shows.

profile *n.* a description of a person that includes his or her most important or noteworthy characteristics.

strict *adj.* having a strong style or approach in handling discipline.